Pebble®

Dogs

Airedale Terriers

by Jody Sullivan Rake

Consulting Editor: Gail Saunders-Smith, PhD

Consultant: Jennifer Zablotny, DVM
Member, American Veterinary Medical Association

Capstone *press*®

Mankato, Minnesota

Pebble Books are published by Capstone Press,
151 Good Counsel Drive, P.O. Box 669, Mankato, Minnesota 56002.
www.capstonepress.com

1 2 3 4 5 6 12 11 10 09 08 07

Library of Congress Cataloging-in-Publication Data
Rake, Jody Sullivan.
    Airedale terriers / by Jody Sullivan Rake.
    p. cm.—(Pebble Books. Dogs)
    Summary: "Simple text and photographs present an introduction to the Airedale
terrier breed, its growth from puppy to adult, and pet care information"—Provided
by publisher.
    Includes bibliographical references and index.
    ISBN-13: 978-1-4296-0808-4 (hardcover)
    ISBN-10: 1-4296-0808-0 (hardcover)
    1. Airedale terrier—Juvenile literature. I. Title. II. Series.
SF429.A6R35 2008
636.755—dc22   2007000894

Note to Parents and Teachers

The Dogs set supports national science standards related to life
science. This book describes and illustrates Airedale terriers.
The images support early readers in understanding the text. The
repetition of words and phrases helps early readers learn new
words. This book also introduces early readers to subject-specific
vocabulary words, which are defined in the Glossary section. Early
readers may need assistance to read some words and to use the
Table of Contents, Glossary, Read More, Internet Sites, and Index
sections of the book.

Table of Contents

Active Airedale Terriers

Airedale terriers
have lots of energy.
They love to run
and swim.

Airedale terriers have
a good sense of smell.
They sniff out
small animals.

From Puppy to Adult

Five to twelve Airedales are born in each litter. Their thick, curly fur is tan and black.

Curious Airedale puppies
enjoy fetching
and exploring.

Adult Airedales are curious and playful too. Bored terriers might chew things that they shouldn't chew.

Airedale terriers are
the largest of all terriers.
Adult Airedales are
half as tall as a desk.

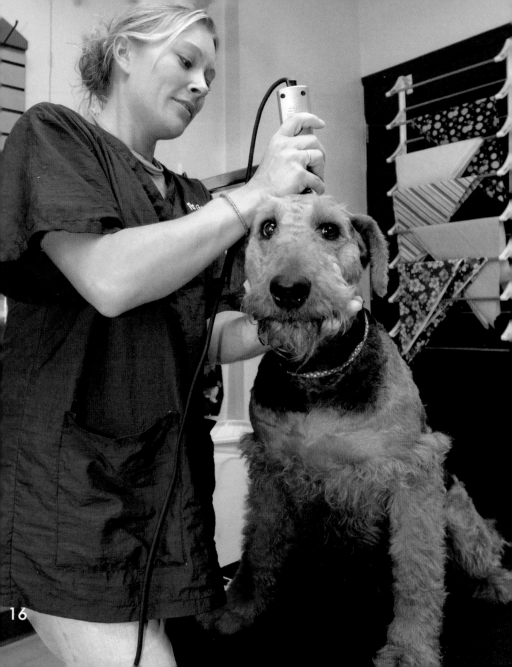

Airedale Terrier Care

Many Airedale terriers have their fur cut. They need to be brushed every day.

Airedale terriers need lots of training. They quickly learn new tricks.

Airedale terriers
are fun, loving pets
that need lots of attention.

Glossary

attention—playing, talking, and spending time with someone or something

bored—not interested in something

curious—excited to find out about something new

energy—the strength to do active things without becoming tired

explore—to go searching or looking around

fetch—to go after something and bring it back

litter—a group of animals born at one time to the same mother

train—to teach an animal how to do something

trick—a clever or skillful act

Read More

Einhorn, Kama. *My First Book About Dogs.* Sesame Subjects. New York: Random House, 2006.

Murray, Julie. *Airedale Terriers.* Dogs. Edina, Minn.: Abdo, 2003.

Internet Sites

FactHound offers a safe, fun way to find Internet sites related to this book. All of the sites on FactHound have been researched by our staff.

Here's how:

1. Visit *www.facthound.com*

2. Choose your grade level.

3. Type in this book ID **1429608080** for age-appropriate sites. You may also browse subjects by clicking on letters, or by clicking on pictures and words.

4. Click on the **Fetch It** button.

FactHound will fetch the best sites for you!

Index

Word Count: 118
Grade: 1
Early-Intervention Level: 14

Editorial Credits

Becky Viaene, editor; Juliette Peters, set designer; Kim Brown, book designer; Kara Birr, photo researcher; Karon Dubke, photographer; Kelly Garvin, photo stylist

Photo Credits

Capstone Press/Karon Dubke, 12, 14, 16, 20; Cheryl A. Ertelt, 18; Corbis/zefa/M. Rutz, 8; iStockphoto/James Boulette, 6; Mark Raycroft, cover, 10; Shutterstock/Iztok Noc, 1; www.jeanmfogle.com, 4

Capstone Press thanks the staff of Vanity Fur in Mankato, Minnesota, for their assistance with this book.